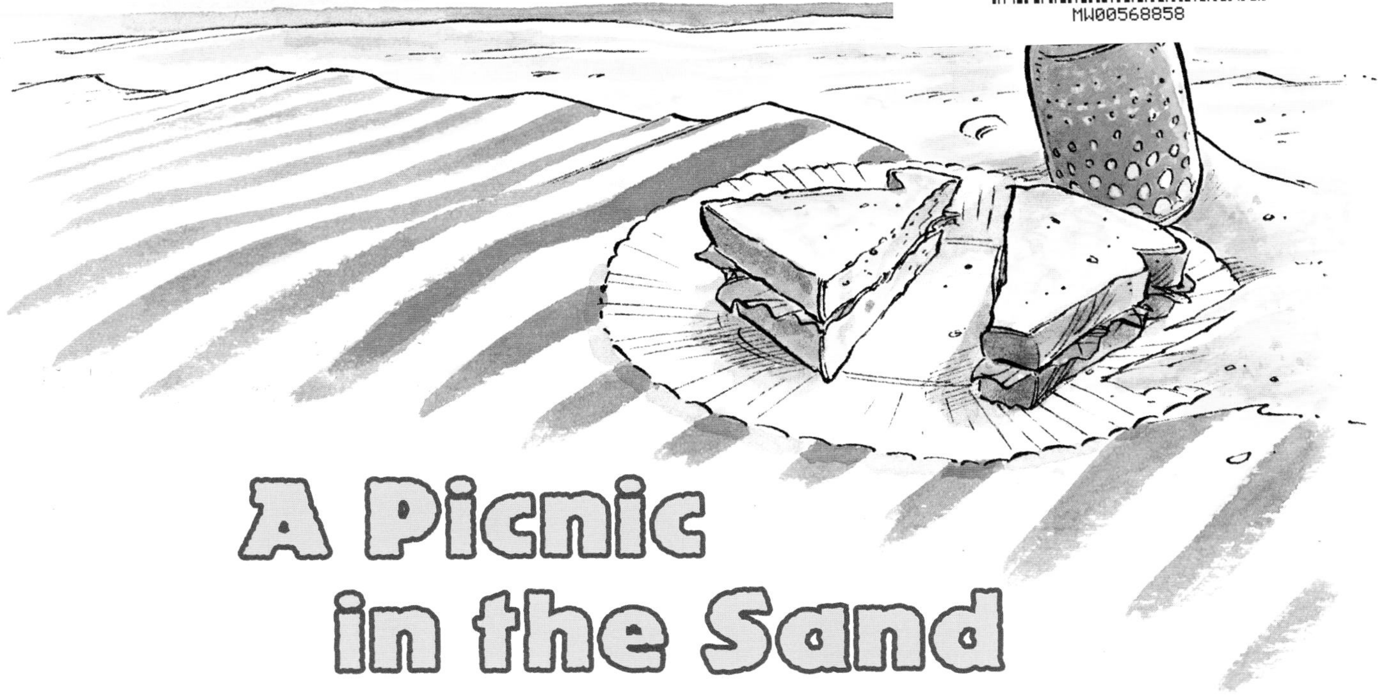

A Picnic in the Sand

Written by Maryann Dobeck
Illustrated by Daniel Vasconcellos

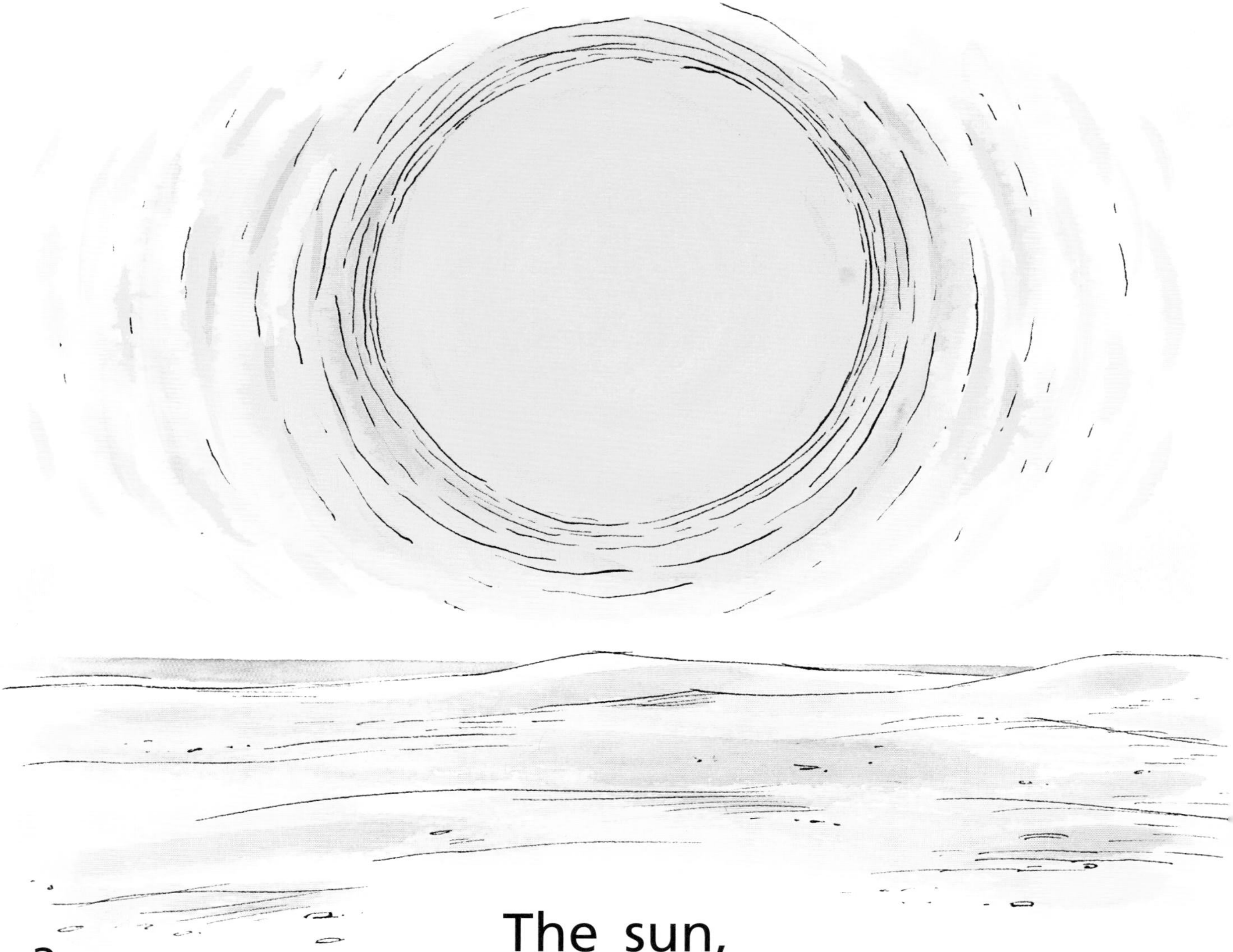

The sun,

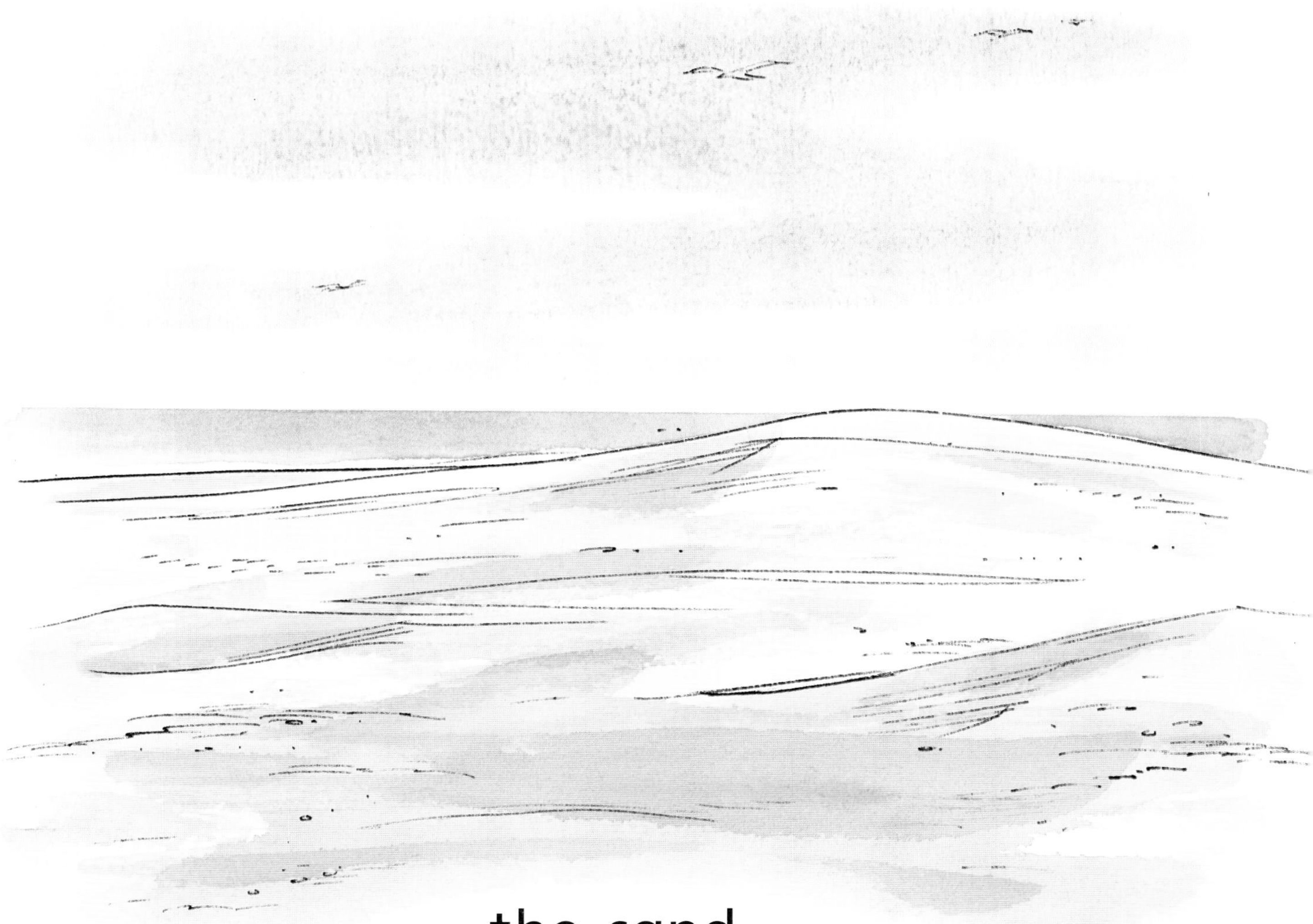

the sand,

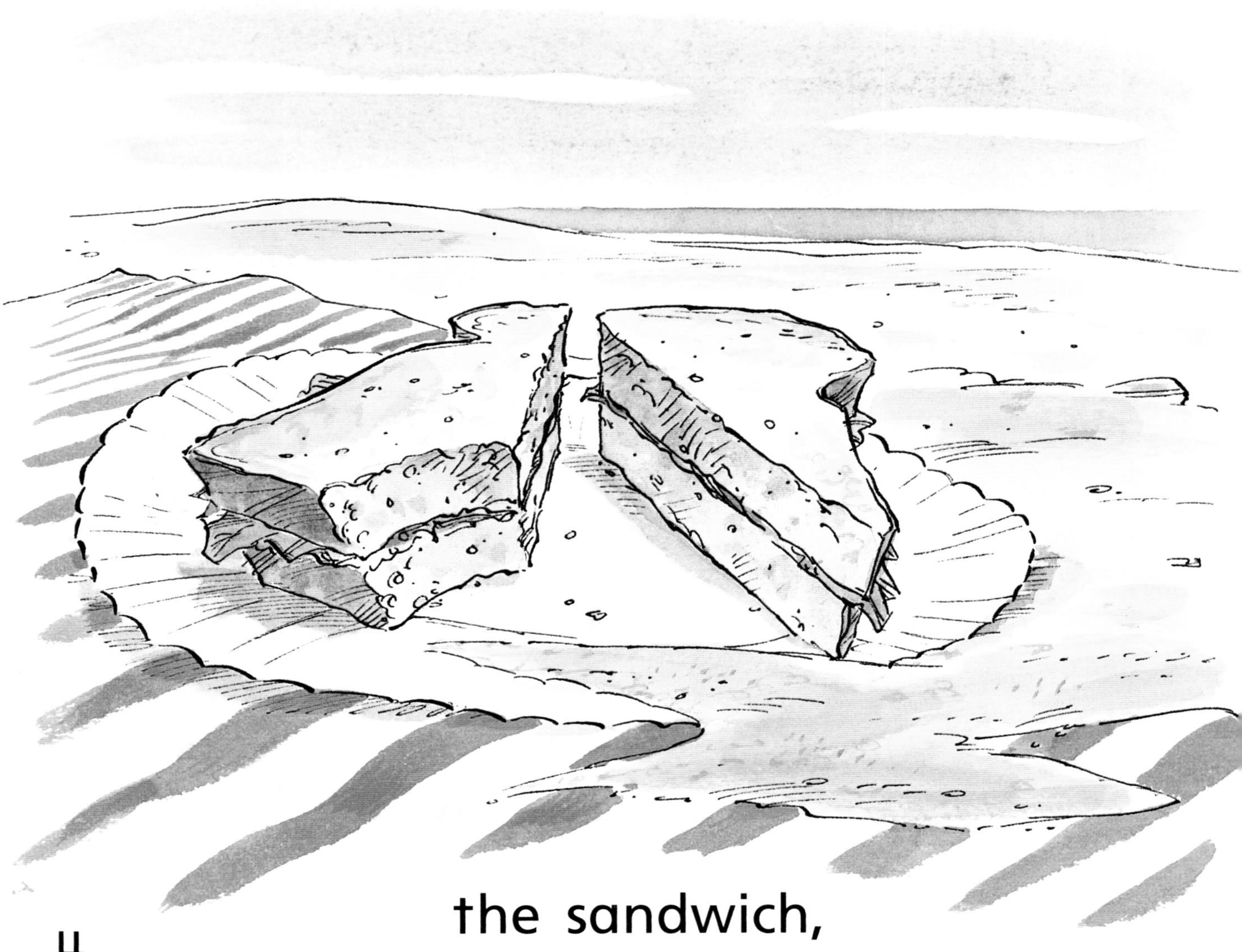

the sandwich,

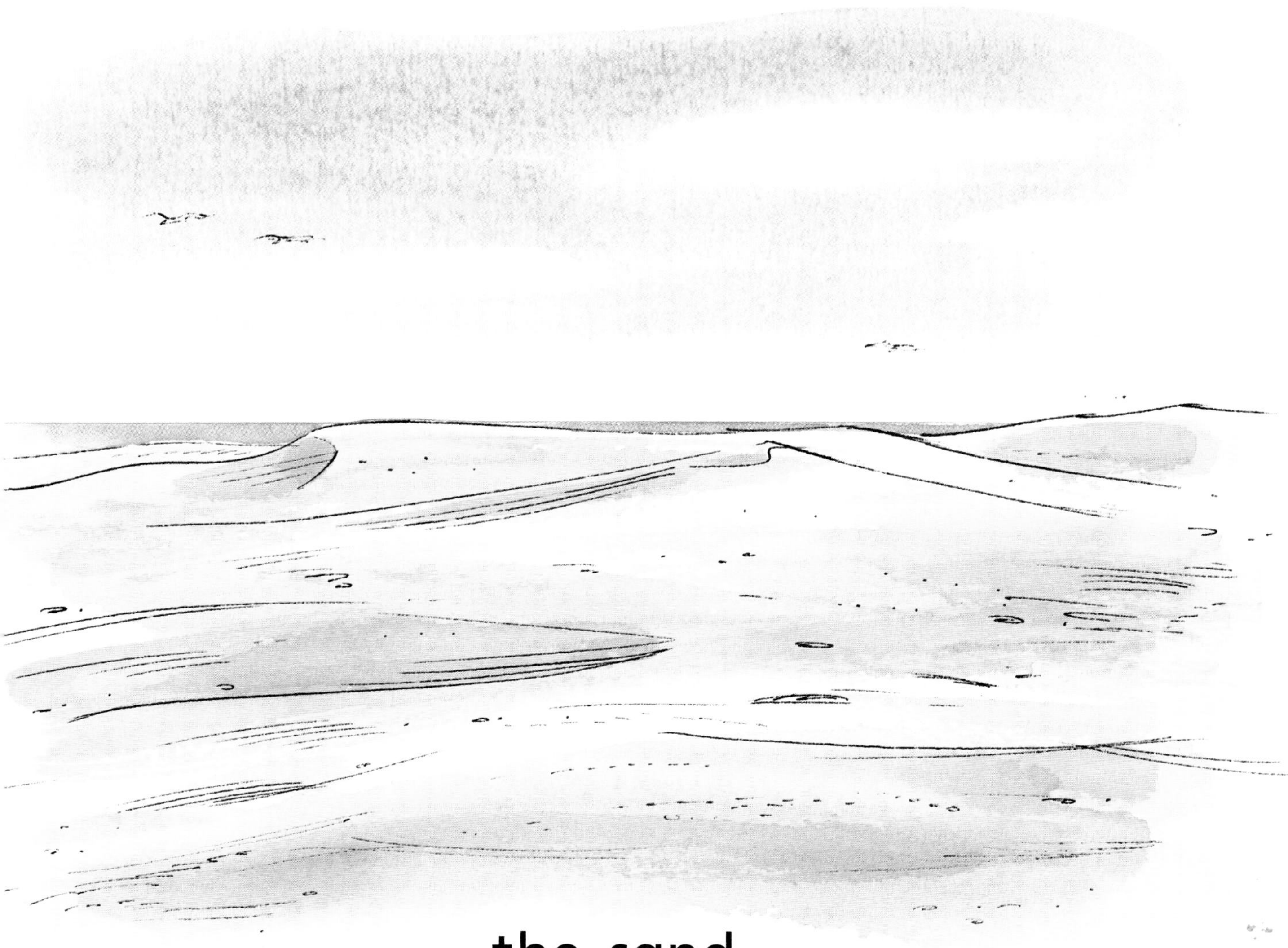

the sand,

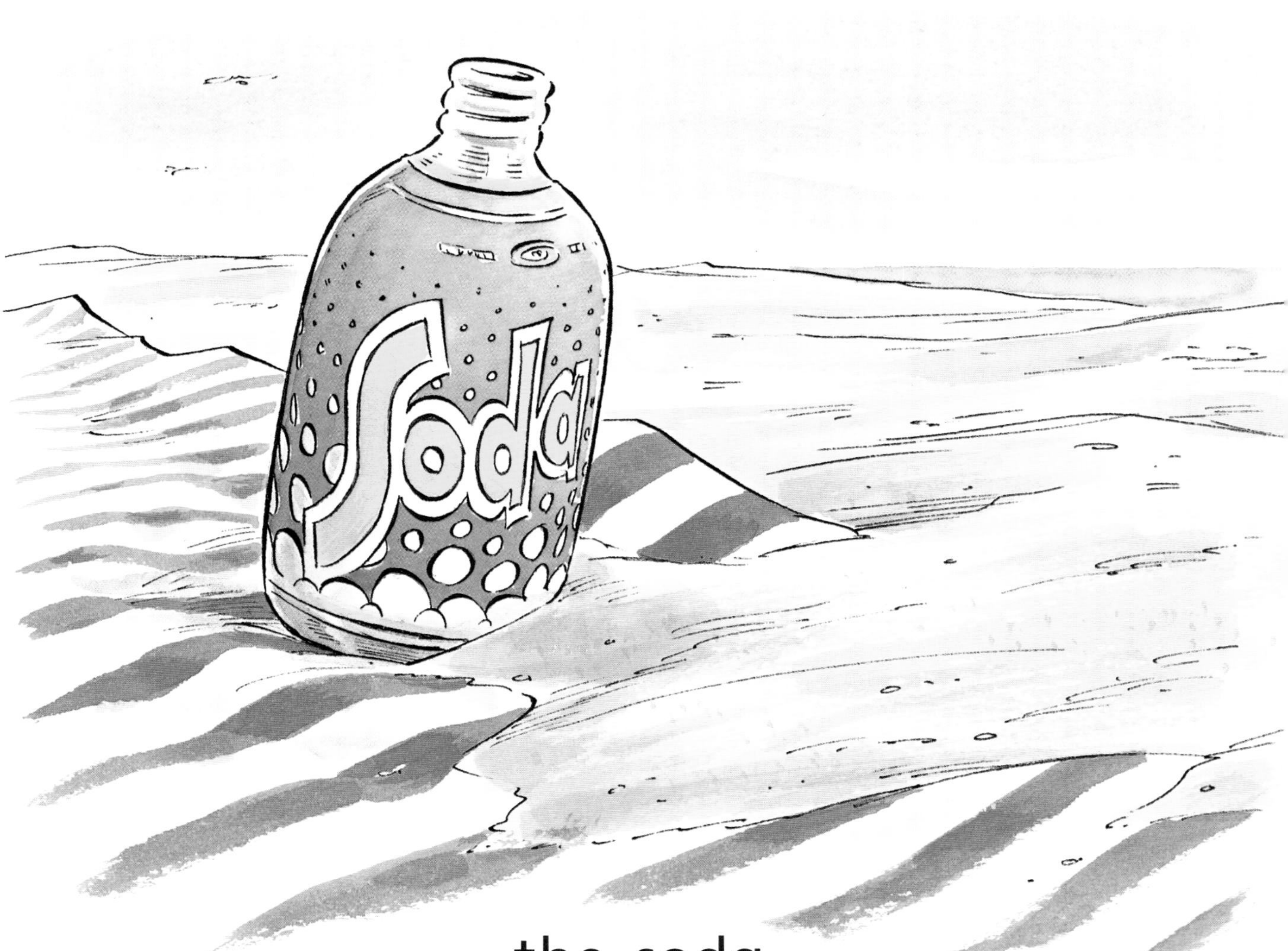

the soda,

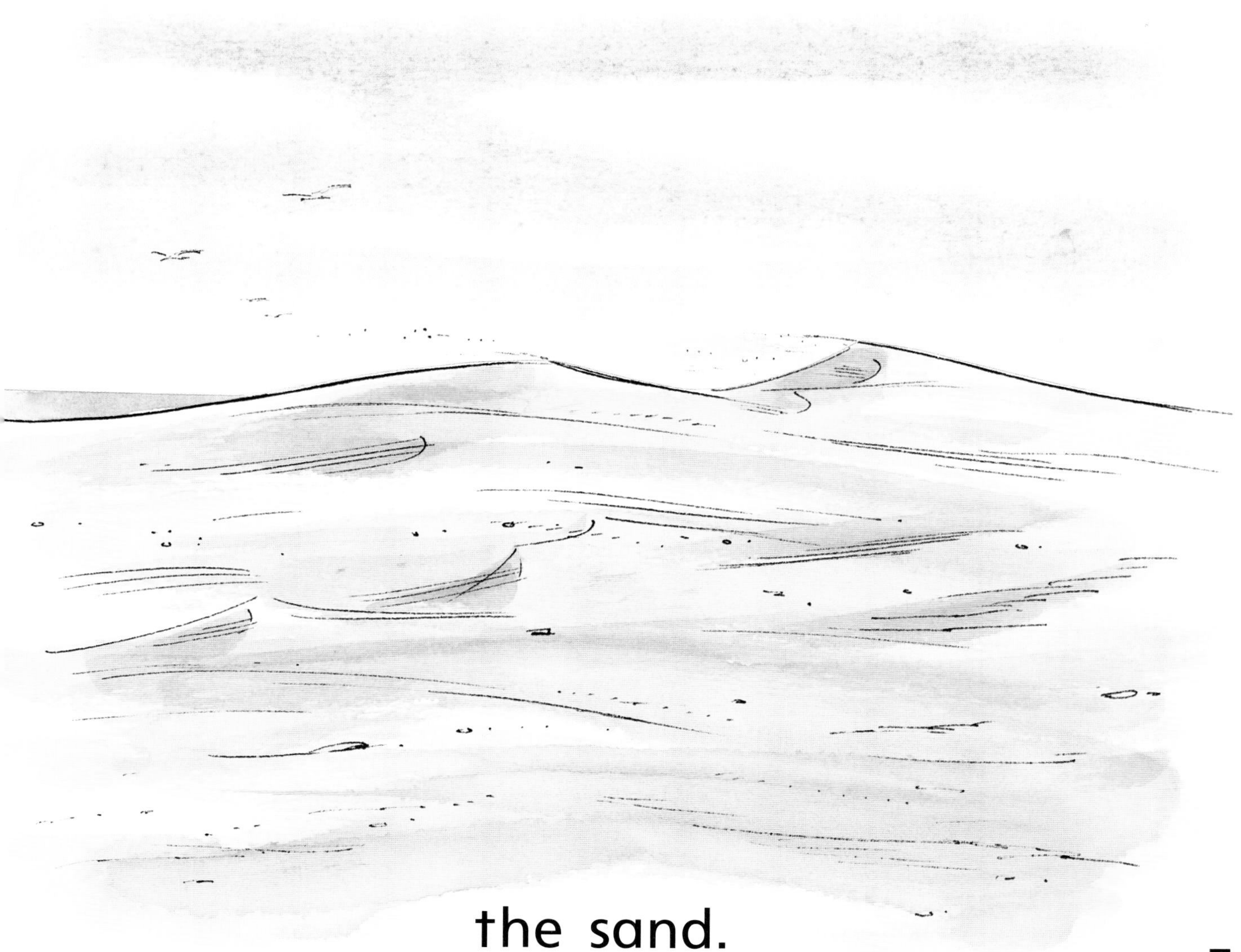

the sand.

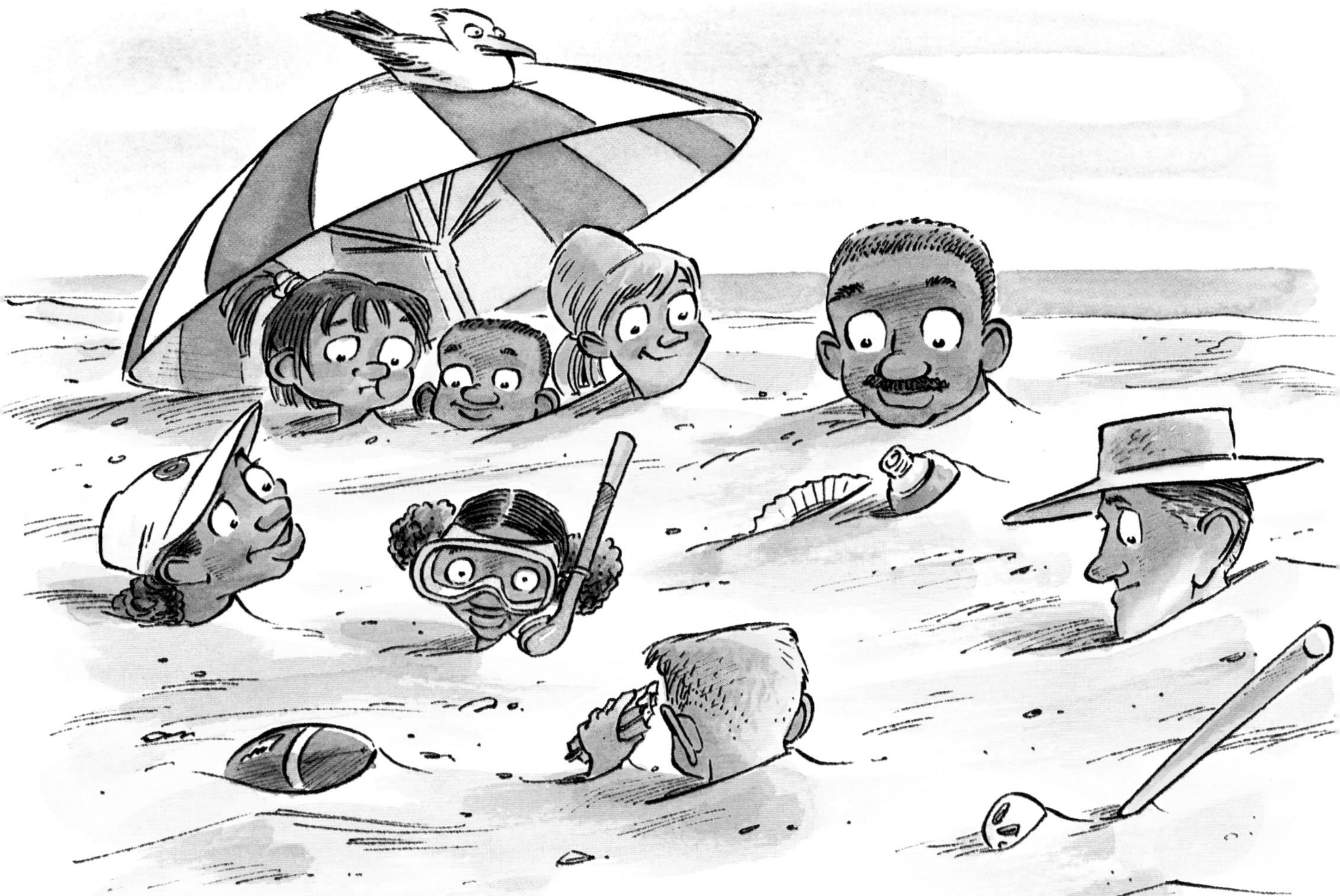

The sand.